ABOVE SYDNEY

AND SURROUNDS

First published in Australia in 2008 by
New Holland Publishers (Australia) Pty Ltd
Sydney • Auckland • London • Cape Town

www.newholland.com.au

1/66 Gibbes Street Chatswood NSW 2067 Australia
218 Lake Road Northcote Auckland New Zealand
86 Edgware Road London W2 2EA United Kingdom
80 McKenzie Street Cape Town 8001 South Africa

National Library of Australia Cataloguing-in-Publication Data:

Tabaka, Richard.
    Above Sydney
    Sydney (NSW). Pictorial works.
    919.44100222
    ISBN 9781741106671 (hbk)

Publisher: Fiona Schultz
Publishing manager: Lliane Clarke
Project editor: Christine Chua
Design: Barbara Cowan
Cover design: Natasha Hayles
Production manager: Linda Bottari
Printer: SNP/Leefung Printing Co Ltd, China

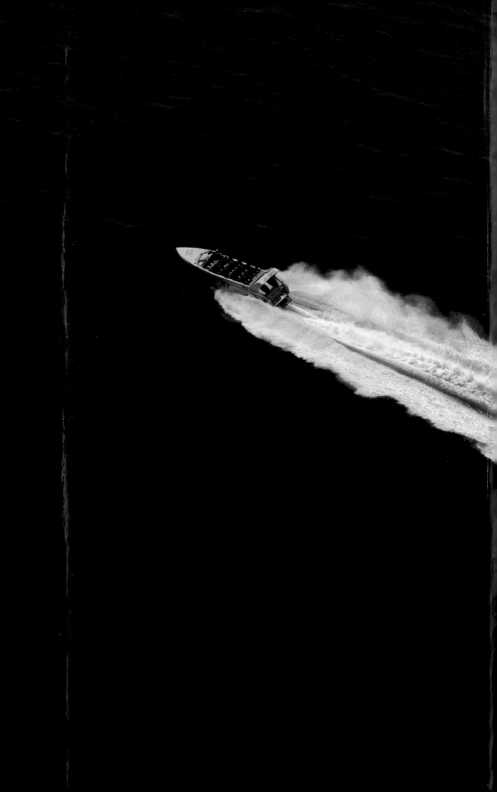

ABOVE SYDNEY
AND SURROUNDS

RICHARD TABAKA

NH
NEW
HOLLAND

Contents

Acknowledgements

I am very grateful to Julie Webber for her support, understanding and patience while waiting lonely at home for flying sessions to conclude.

I should like to take this opportunity to thank the following individuals for their help and support:
Peter Wilson from Airscape for teaching me to fly safely,
Margaret Nightingale, David Rittie, Steve Coen and Mike from Sport Aircraft Club at Wedderburn for allowing me to use the club facility,
Colin Evans and Float Trikes Australia for flying me around Sydney Harbour,
David Rolfe and John Taru from the Oaks aerodrome for their hospitality,
Rodney Hay for the use of the hangar and office during my prolonged stay at the Katoomba airfield,
Len Birger and Kevin Magennis from Somersby airfield for their help,
Eva and Janusz Pendel for their hospitality in Sydney.

Very special thanks to my best friends Maja and Peter Orczykowski for letting me use their beautiful house as my second home.

Sydney is in a coastal basin bordered by the Pacific Ocean to the east, the Blue Mountains to the west, the Hawkesbury River to the north and the Royal National Park to the south. Sydney lies on a submergent coastline, where the ocean level has risen to flood deep river valleys carved in the Hawkesbury sandstone. One of these drowned valleys, Port Jackson, better known as Sydney Harbour, is the largest natural harbour in the world. There are more than 70 harbour and ocean beaches, including the famous Bondi Beach and Manly Beach, in the urban area.

Geographically, Sydney sprawls over two major regions: the Cumberland Plain, a relatively flat region lying to the south and west of the harbour, and the Hornsby Plateau, a sandstone plateau lying mainly to the north of the harbour, dissected by steep valleys. The oldest parts of the city are located in the flat areas south of the harbour; the North Shore was slower to develop because of its hilly topography, and was mostly a quiet backwater until the Sydney Harbour Bridge opened in 1932, linking it to the rest of the city.

The Opera House with the Sydney CBD in the background
Pages 2–3: A Sydney Jet cutting water on Sydney Harbour

North Sydney skyline
Pages 6–7: A panoramic view of Sydney

Sydney CBD skyline from the north

North Sydney—view towards Milsons Point and the Harbour Bridge

Government House in the gardens of The Domain and the Sydney skyline

Bradfield Highway approaching the Sydney Harbour Bridge

The Domain with the Finger Wharf Apartments at Woolloomooloo
Facing page: The Sydney Opera House on Bennelong Point

16

Neutral Bay against the North Sydney backdrop

Kurraba Point

Kirribilli House, the Prime Minister's official residence in Sydney

Kirribilli Wharf

Above and facing page: The Old Quarantine Station. It was here that white Australia's convict heritage began and incoming migrants were welcomed (and quarantined) inside Sydney Heads.

Right and facing page: HMAS Sydney memorial at Bradleys Head

The Naval Depot, Garden Island

Darling Point, Sydney Harbour

Fort Denison (facing page) is a former penal site and defensive facility occupying a small island located north of the Royal Botanical Gardens in Sydney Harbour. Prior to European settlement, the island had the Aboriginal name Mat-te-wan-ye. After the first fleet arrived in 1788, Governor Phillip and his Advocate-General used the name Rock Island. In 1788, a convict named Thomas Hill was sentenced to a week on bread and water in irons and the island came to be known as Pinchgut. Once a 15-metre high sandstone rock, the island was flattened as prisoners under the command of Captain George Barney, the civil engineer for the colony, quarried it for sandstone to construct nearby Circular Quay.

Shark Island (left) lies offshore of the suburbs of Point Piper, Rose Bay and Vaucluse. The aboriginal peoples call the island Boambilly. The name Shark Island is from its shape, which is said to resemble a shark. Parts were set aside as a recreation reserve as early as 1879 and it was also used as an animal quarantine station and naval depot up until 1975. At that time it became exclusively a recreation reserve and part of the Sydney Harbour National Park.

Clark Island (page 28) lies offshore of the suburb of Darling Point. The island derives its name from Lieutenant Ralph Clark of the First Fleet, who maintained a vegetable garden on the island. Today the island is uninhabited, and forms part of the Sydney Harbour National Park.

Two views of Shark Island, Sydney Harbour

Ford Denison, Sydney Harbour

Clark Island, Sydney Harbour

Rushcutters Bay, Sydney Harbour

Vaucluse style of living

Kincoppal-Rose Bay, School of the Sacred Heart, Vaucluse

Manly as seen from above Sydney Harbour

South Head with Hornsby Lighthouse

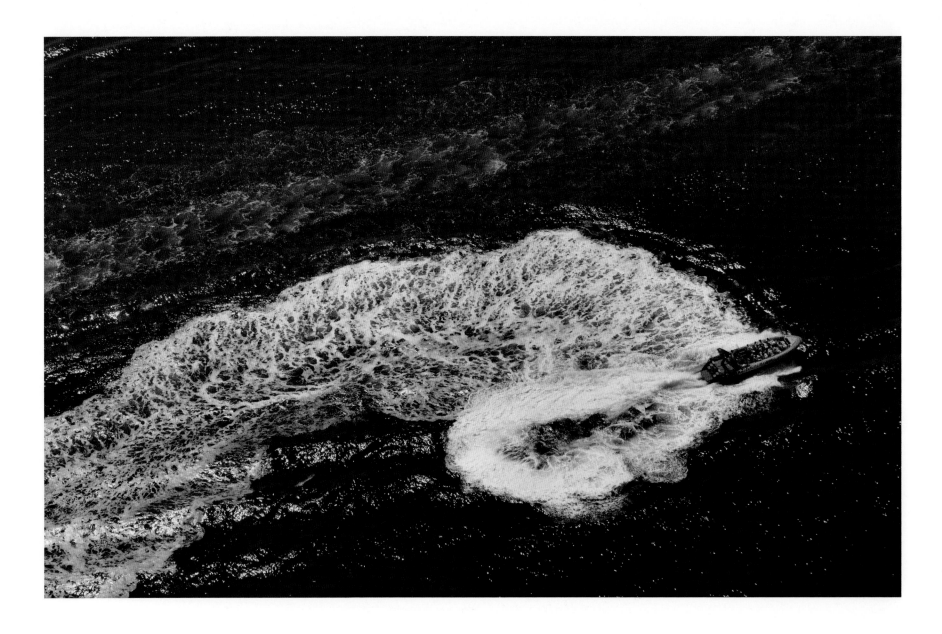

Sydney Jet—the speed boat entertaining passengers on Sydney Harbour

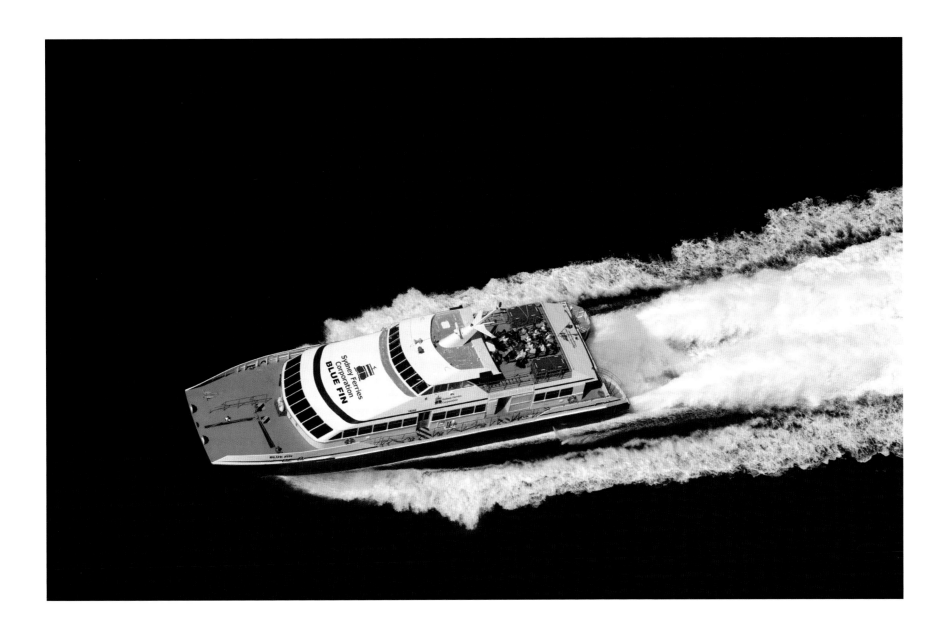

Blue Fin catamaran, Sydney Ferries

Mooring boats at Careel Bay

Water skiers on the Parramatta River

Two motor boats cutting the waters of Broken Bay,
north of Ku-Ring-Gai Chase National Park

Parramatta River near Gladesville Bridge with Hunters Hill in the distance

Riverfront apartments at Drummoyne

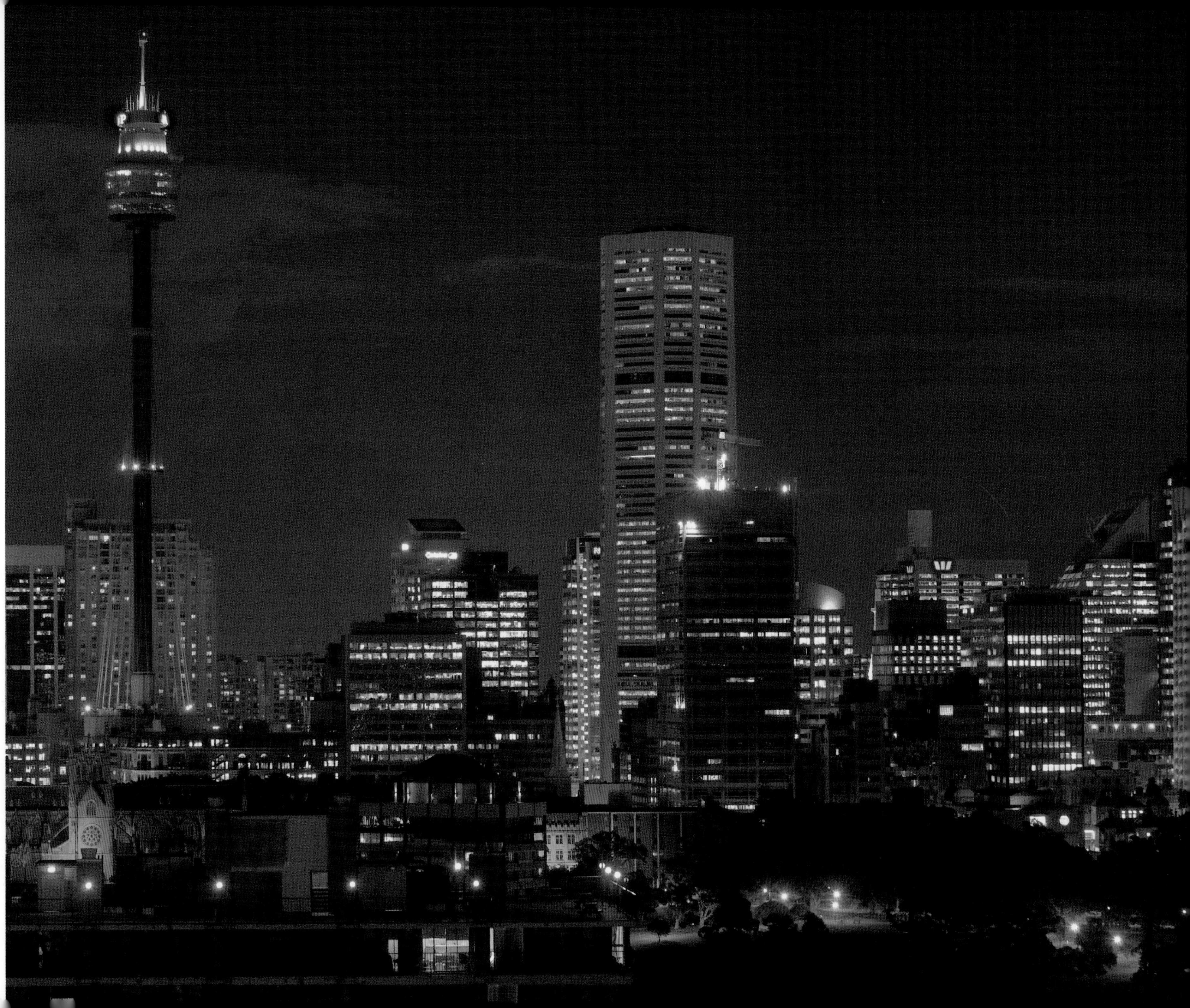

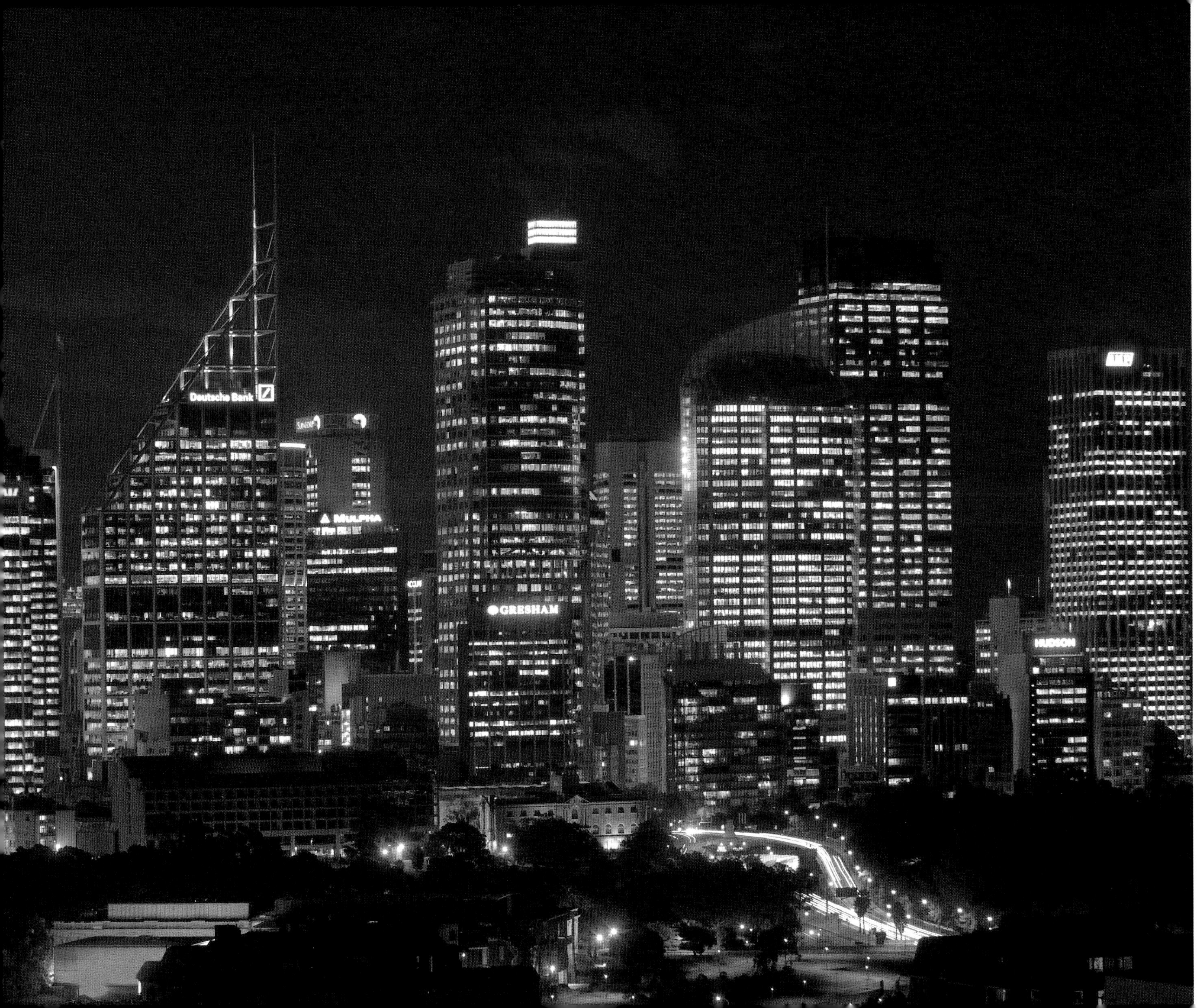
Deutsche Bank
MULPHA
GRESHAM
HUDSON

The jewels of Sydney Harbour—the Opera House and the Harbour Bridge at night

Dining at Potts Point cafe
Pages 40–41: Sydney CBD at night
from Potts Point

The Sydney Tower at twilight

Golden pillars of the Harbour Bridge as seen from Five Dock

Twilight view of the city from Pyrmont

Evening traffic from the Anzac Bridge

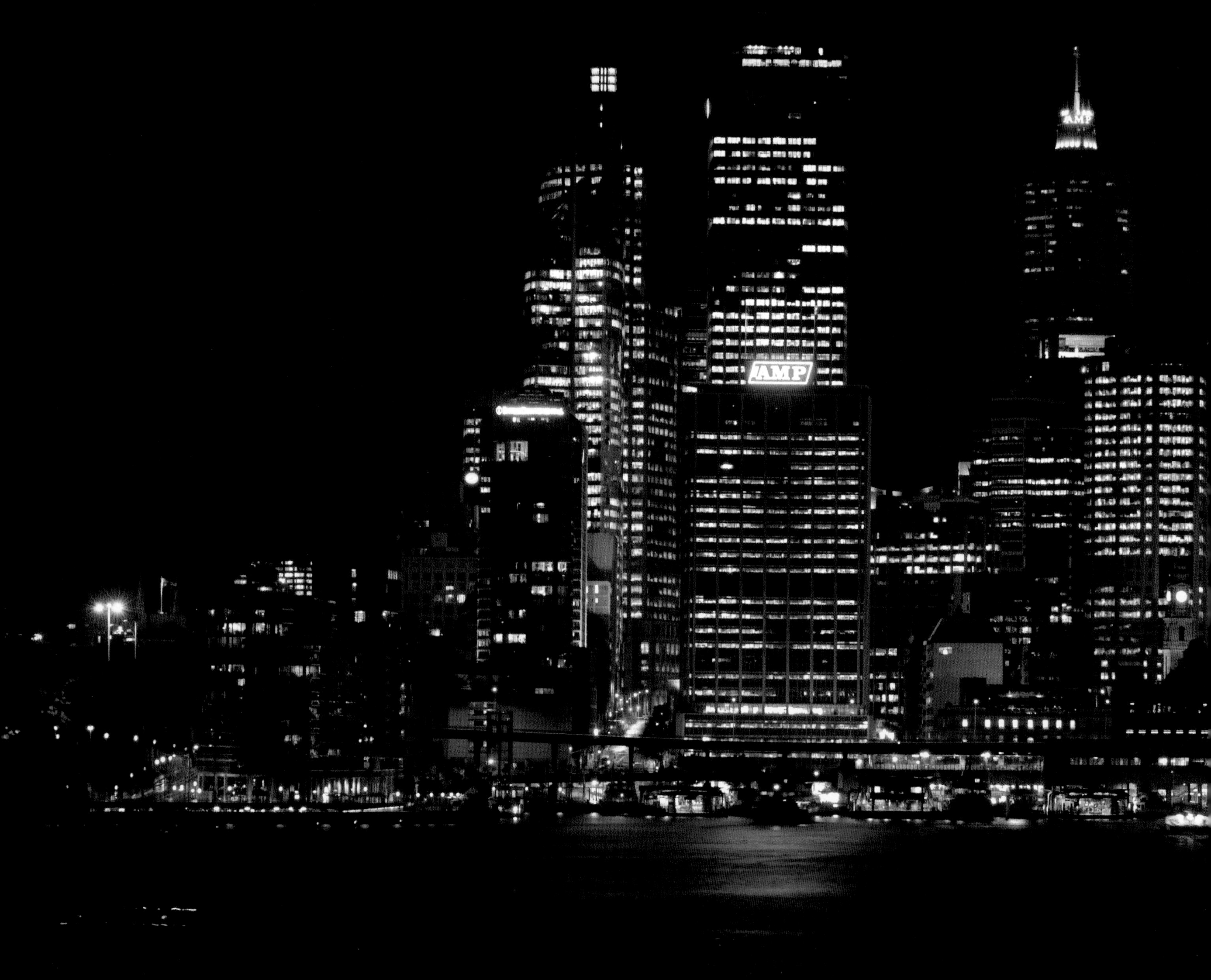
AMP
AMP

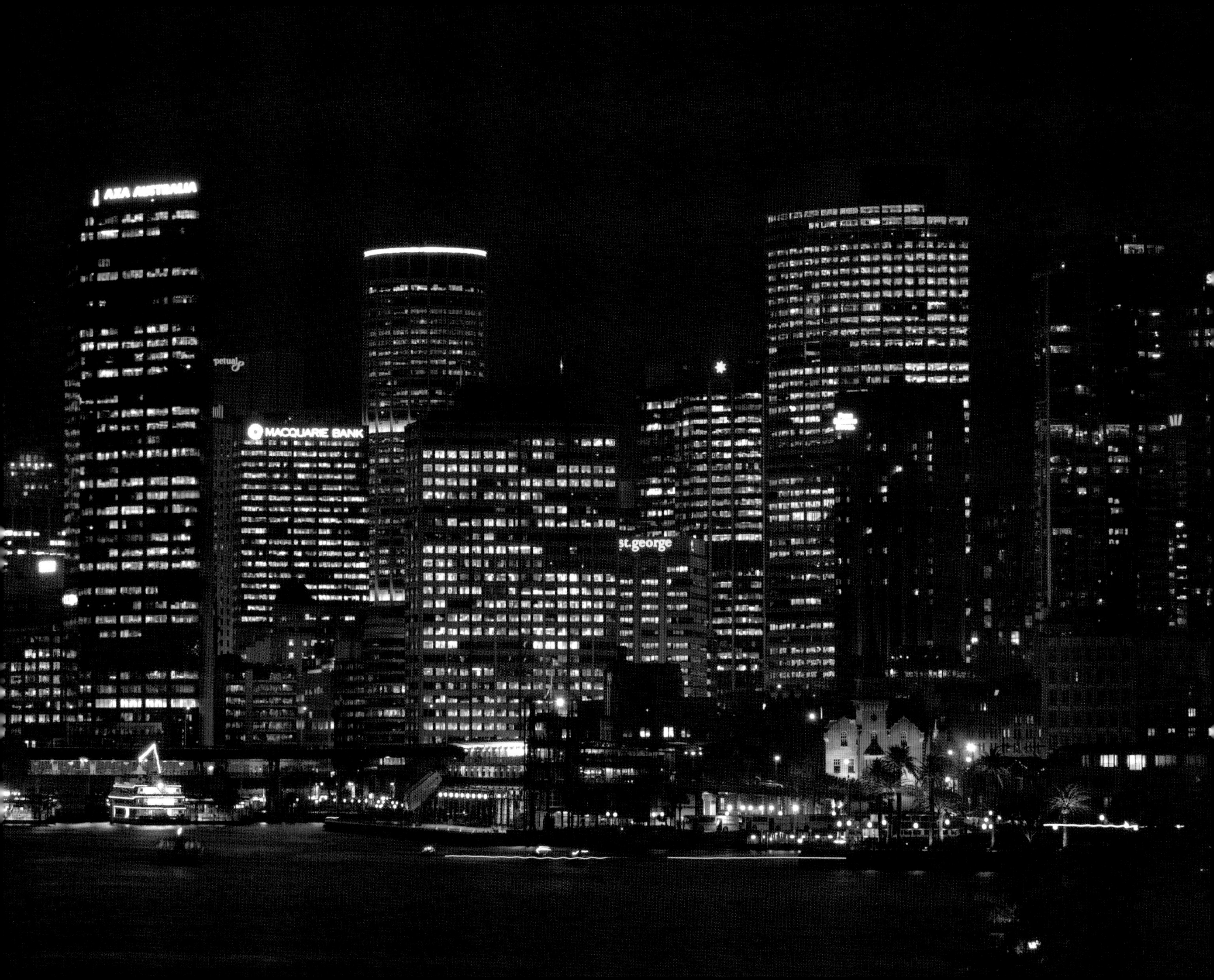
AXA AUSTRALIA
MACQUARIE BANK
st.george

Golden reflections at dusk as seen from Pyrmont

Pages 48–49: Circular Quay and Sydney CBD at night

The Anzac Bridge

Sydney CBD's skyline as seen from Five Dock

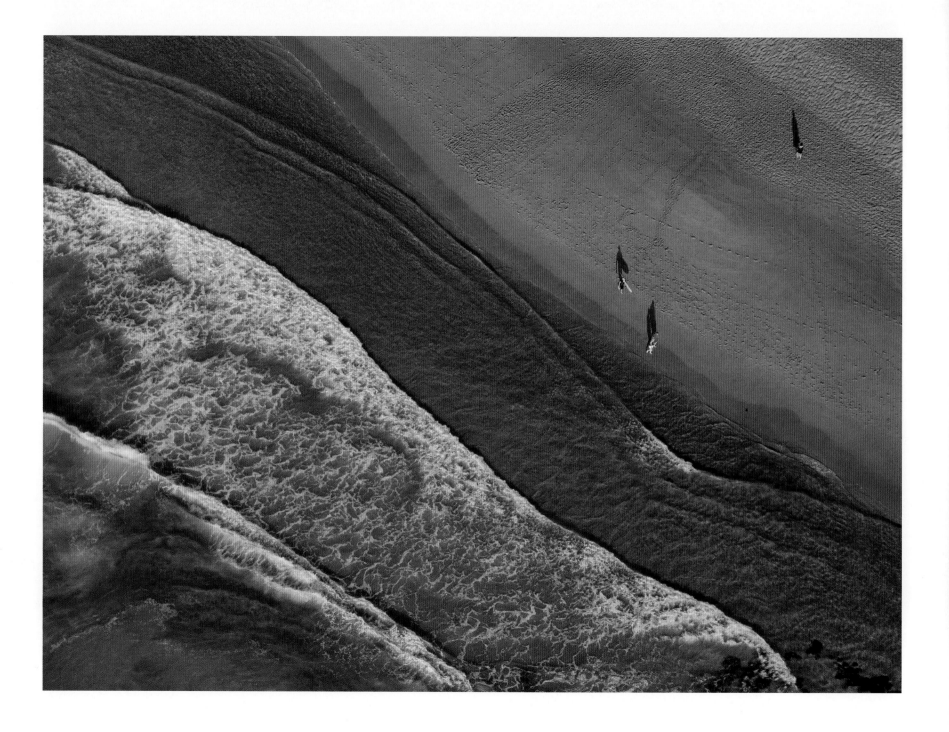

Waiting for fish, Bungan Head
Page 54: Morning joggers on Bungan Beach, Newport

Rocky shore on the Northern Beaches
Page 55: Long Reef Point

Little Reef off Bungan Head

Turimetta Head, Warriewood

Pages 60–77: There are over 20 surf beaches along Sydney's metropolitan seashore, which attract droves of Sydneysiders to surf, jog and swim or just to admire the morning light, waves and patterns created by rocks and sand submerging in crystal clear waters.

Dee Why Head, North Curl Curl

Rock Bath at Dee Why Head, North Curl Curl

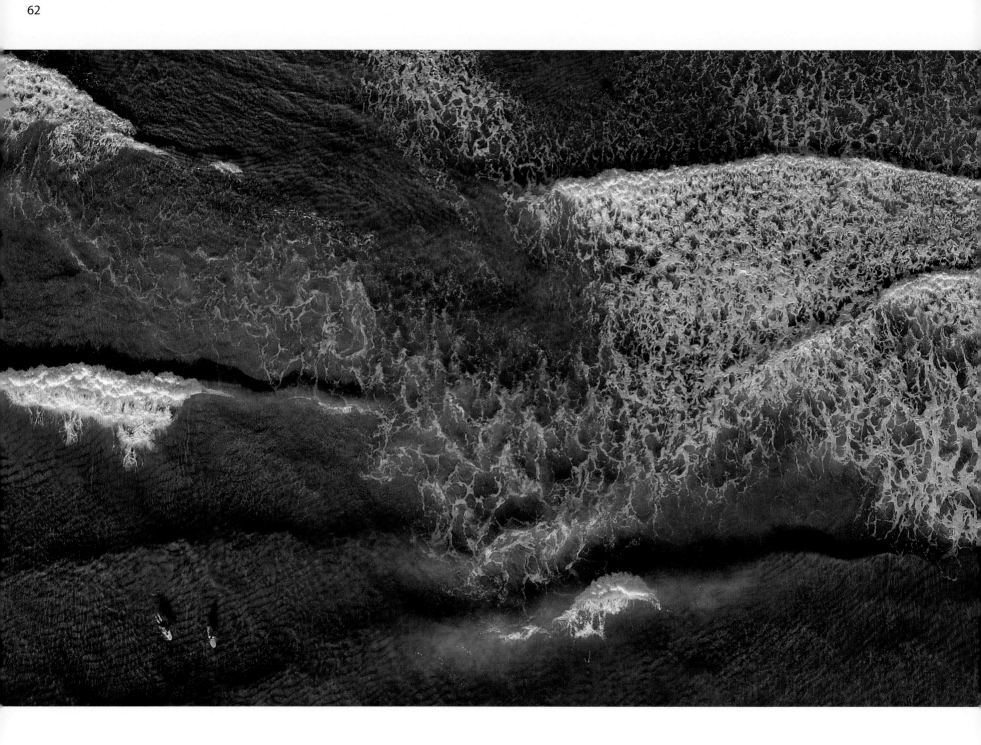

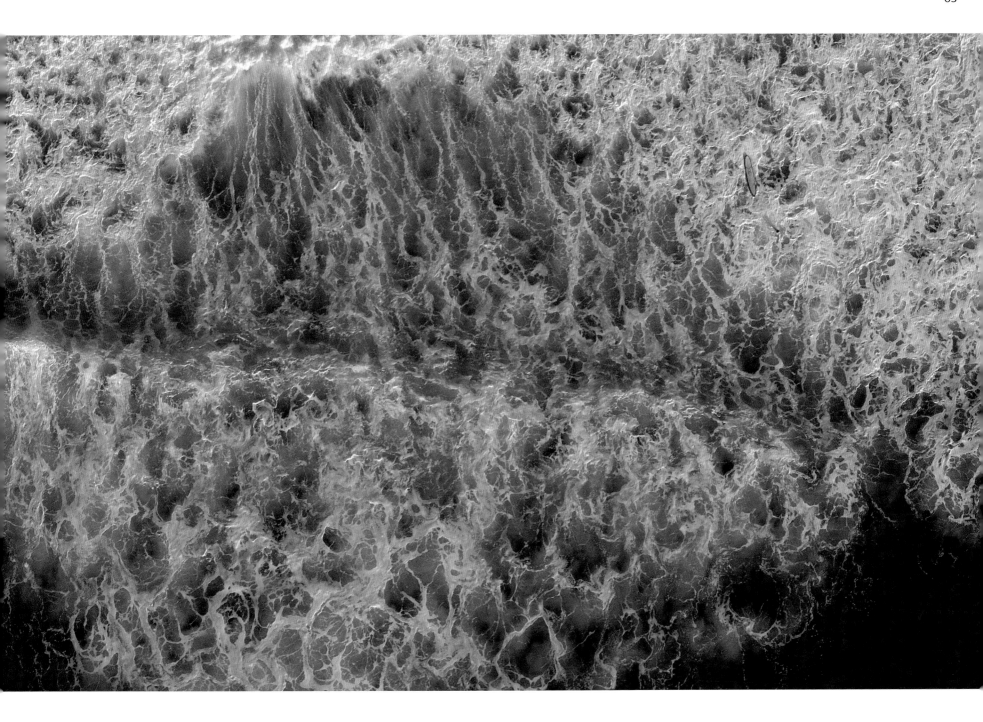

70

Surfboats racing at Manly Beach at an inter-club surf lifesaving carnival to hone the fitness, skills and drills of lifesavers

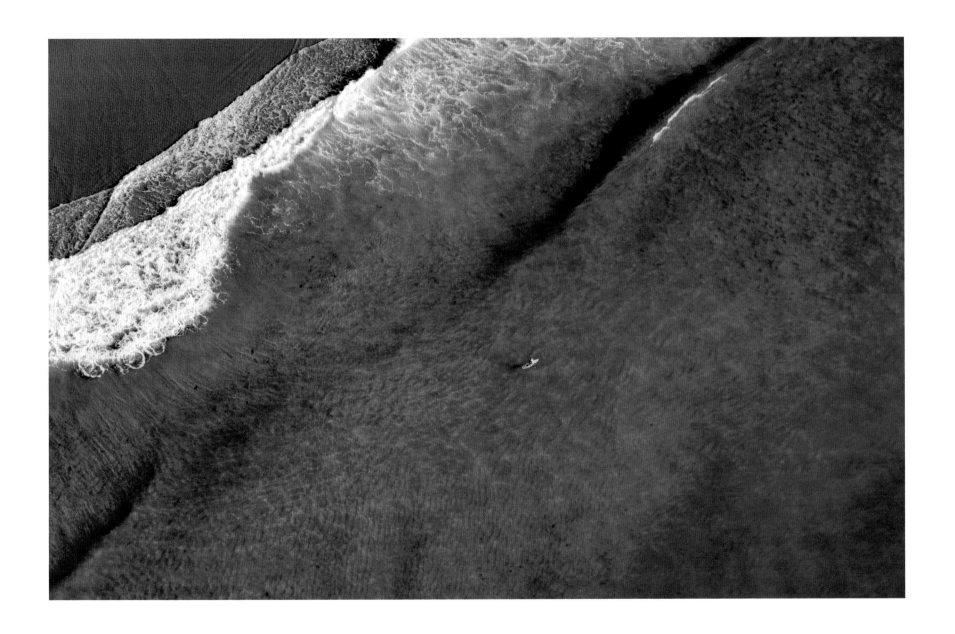

Above and facing page: Palm Beach, the most northerly beach in Sydney

Northern Beaches architecture
Facing page: Little Head and Whale Beach

Bilgola Beach Rock Pool

Warriewood Beach and Turimetta Head

Long Reef
Facing page: Long Reef Golf Course

Bungan Beach

Narrabeen Beach

Above and facing page: The Mona Vale Rock Pool

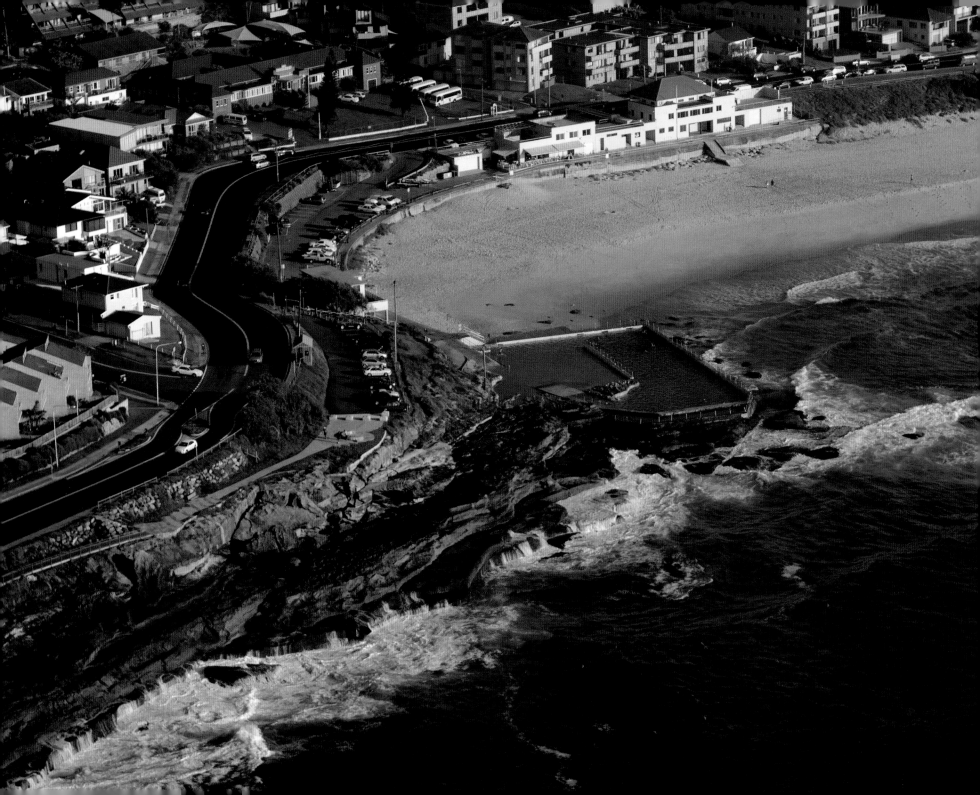

Rocky cliffs along North Curl Curl
Page 90: Rock pool at Curl Curl Beach

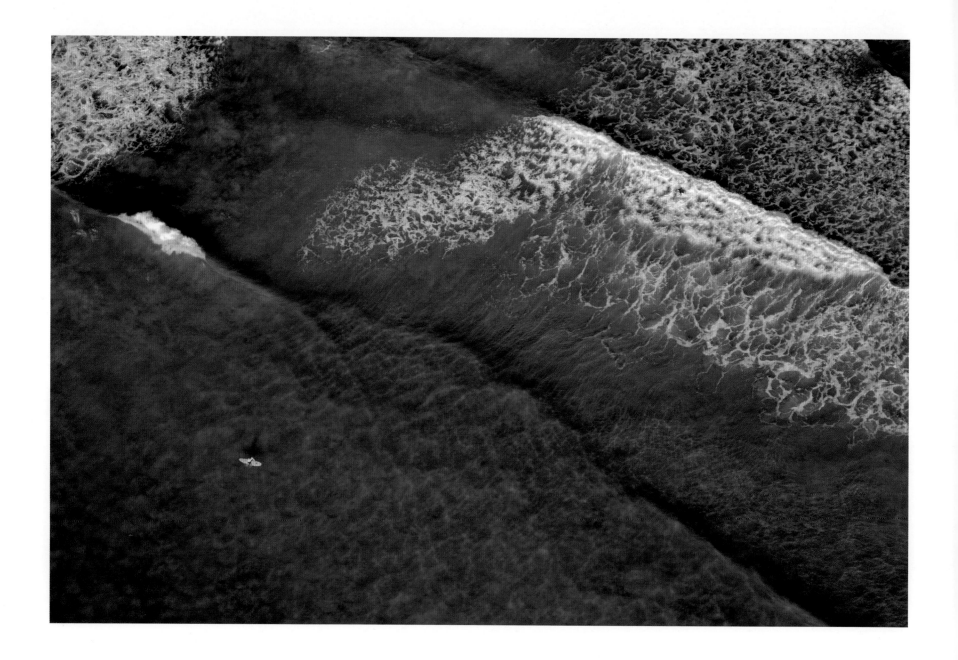

Above and facing page: Manly Beach

St Patrick's Seminary, Manly was the leading seminary of the Australian Catholic Church from its foundation in 1889 to its closure in 1995.

Manly with view of Manly Cove, Middle Harbour and Sydney CBD in the distance

... (image data)

Ben Buckler and Bondi Beach

Waverley Cemetery at Bronte

The heads of peninsula; Barrenjoey, West and Middle with Lion Island in the centre as seen from above Woy Woy

Hawkesbury River covered in morning fog

Barrenjoey Head and the lighthouse are the landmarks of the northern tip of the Sydney coastline

Pittwater with two Royal Yacht Clubs dominating the water landscape

Scotland Island on Pittwater

Secluded marinas in bays of Ku-Ring-Gai Chase National Park

The Hawkesbury River as seen from above Broken Bay

Brooklyn Bridge over the Hawkesbury River with a view towards the ocean

Marsden Park at Campbelltown

A residential development in the western Sydney suburb of Penrith

Newington, the site of the Athletes Village for the 2000 Sydney Olympics, has quickly become a major residential suburb.
Facing page: Cecil Hills at Liverpool

Sydney International
Regatta Centre, Penrith

Sydney Olympic Park is a 640-hectare site located in the suburb of Homebush Bay. It was built for the 2000 Olympics and continues to be used for sporting and cultural events, including the Sydney Royal Easter Show, Sydney Festival, Big Day Out and a number of world class sporting fixtures. It is served by the Olympic Park railway line and station. There are also regular ferry services to the nearby wharf which run to and from various points around Sydney Harbour.

Before its transformation, a large part of Olympic Park was an industrial wasteland after more than a century of industrial and military ventures on the site. The site was once home to a brickworks, abattoir and an armaments depot as well as being the site for eight of Sydney's rubbish dumps.

With the successful completion of the 2000 Olympics, Sydney Olympic Park has undergone a significant amount of development work to support its conversion to a multipurpose facility with a number of businesses re-locating to the area.

Penrith Whitewater Stadium is an artificial whitewater sporting facility which hosted the canoe/kayak slalom events at the 2000 Sydney Olympics. The facility is part of the Penrith Lakes Scheme, and is adjacent to the Sydney International Regatta Centre.

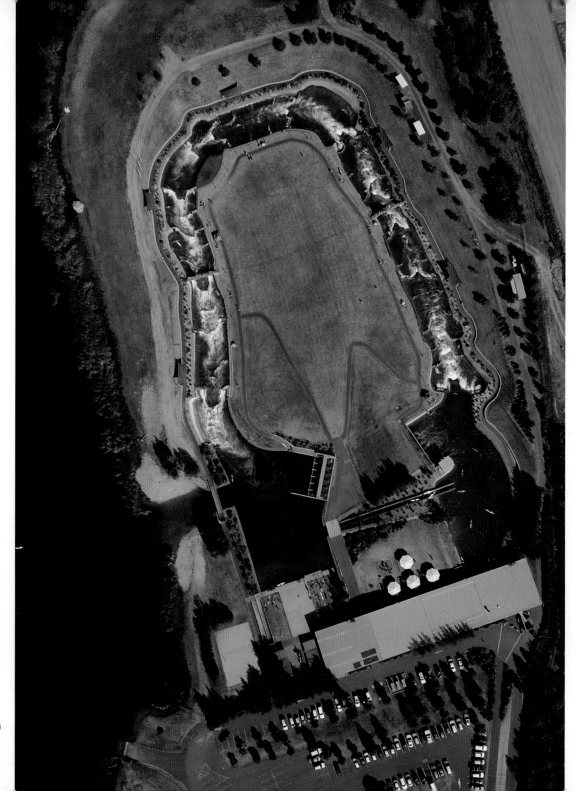

Whitewater Rafting Course, Penrith

ANZ Stadium

Sydney Athletic and Aquatic Centres

The Dome Hall with three
Pavillion Halls and the
Olympic Park Railway Station

Royal National Park in the morning haze, south of Sydney

A rainy view towards Sydney from above Tumbledown Ridge, Nattai

Above and pages 119–122: The four freshwater lakes—Nepean, Avon, Cordeaux and Cataract—hide in a quiet patch of forest and deep gorges. The lakes, part of the water supply reserve for Sydney, are among the last undisturbed systems in the region.

The Cataract Dam, built in 1926 to provide water for the growing population of Sydney, is the first and oldest of the great dams of the Upper Nepean River.

The morning light filters through clouds over Port Kembla

Pages 129–131: Appin Colliery

131

Above and pages 133–134: Port Kembla Steelworks

Wetherill Park, an industrial estate

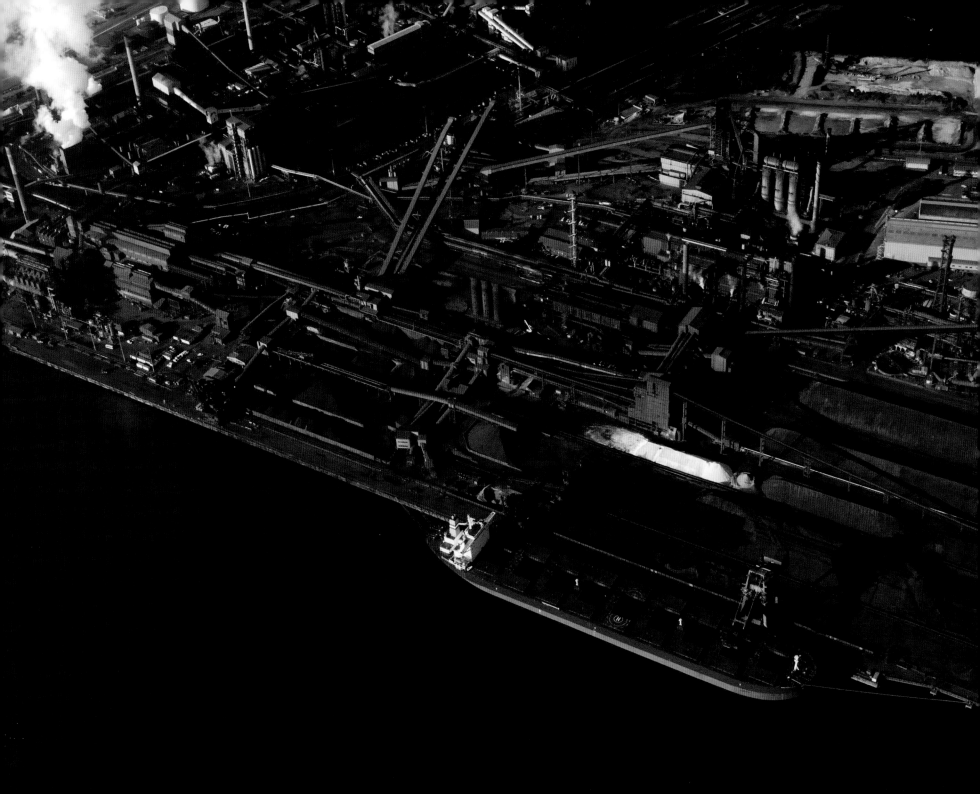

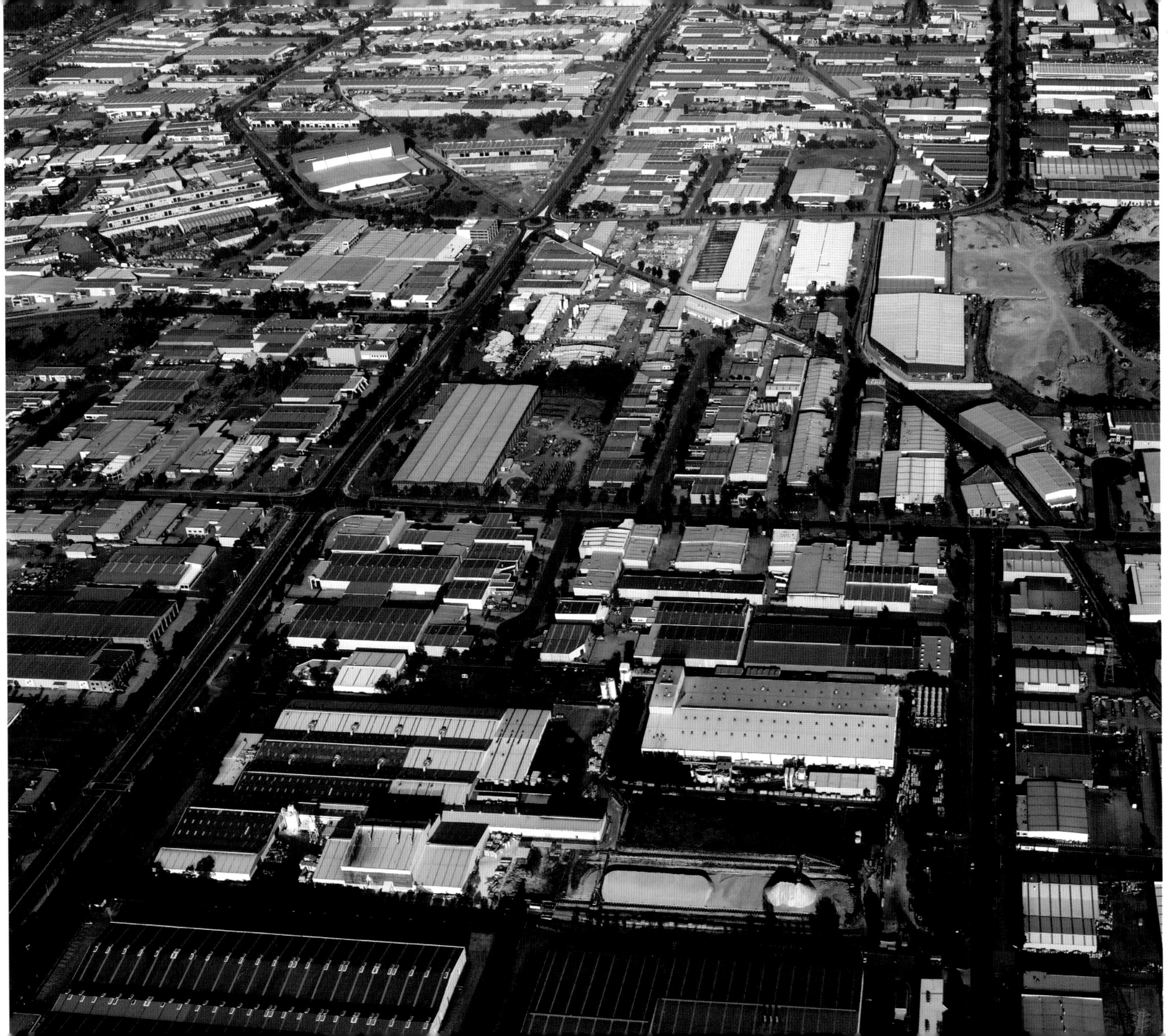

Above and left: The industrial landscape of Wetherill Park

Above and pages 140–149: Situated on the headwaters of the Nepean and Georges Rivers, the Macarthur region is an important agricultural area with rich basalt soils and magnificent gardens.

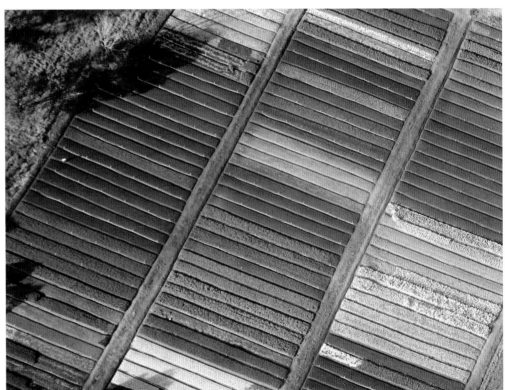

148

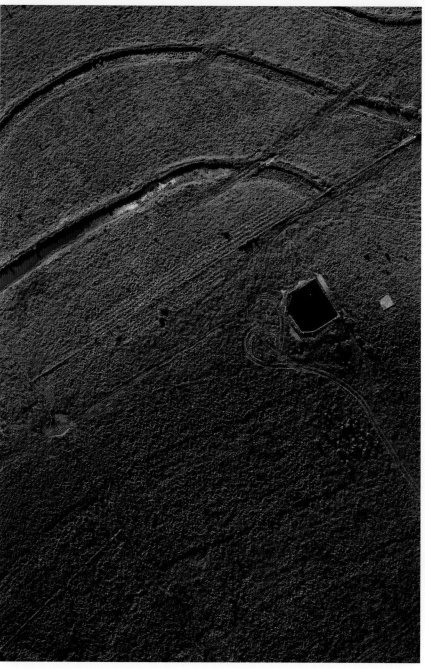

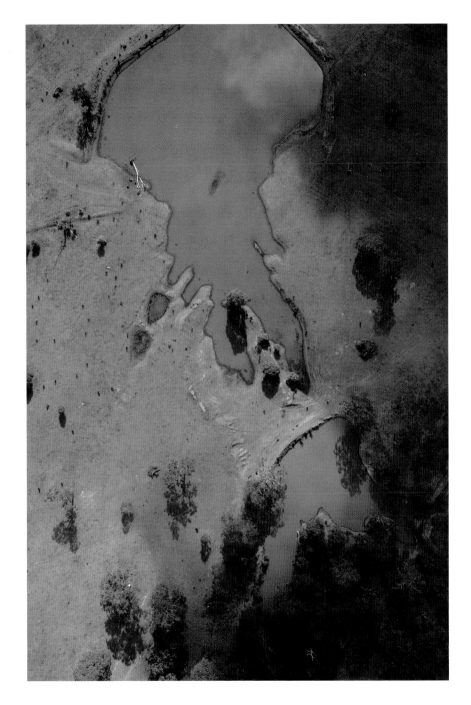

50

Wollongong in the early morning

Wollongong is the third largest city in the state of New South Wales. Located on the coast, 82km south of Sydney, it is known locally as the 'Gong'.

The area, with its history of coal mining and steelworks production, has an industrial port.

From Wollongong to Port Hacking, the full coastal length is composed mostly of the cliffs reaching a height of nearly 200m in places. These cliffs are punctuated by a number of fine, sandy beaches open to the ocean and providing fine swimming and surfing. Several of the beaches can be reached by road, others only by several hours of bush walking.

Pages 152–153: The residential suburbs of Wollongong

The Sea Cliff Bridge, north of Wollongong

Above and page 156: The ocean shore along Royal National Park with Providential Head in the foreground, south of Sydney

Entrance to Lake Illawara

Above and facing page: Wattamolla Beach in the Royal National Park

Rocky shore north of Wattamolla Beach

Little Marley and Big Marley Beaches with Port Hacking Point in the distance

Above and facing page: Coastal sand and water patterns

The interchange Great Western Highway and M7

Commuters on Warringah Freeway, North Sydney

The Sea Cliff Bridge near Wollongong

The interchange of Hume Highway and Narellan Road near Campbelltown

Right and facing page: Nan Tien Buddhist Temple at Barkeley near Wollongong

Hindu Temple near Helensburgh
Facing page: Al-Musjit Bait-Ul-Huda Mosque, Marsden Park

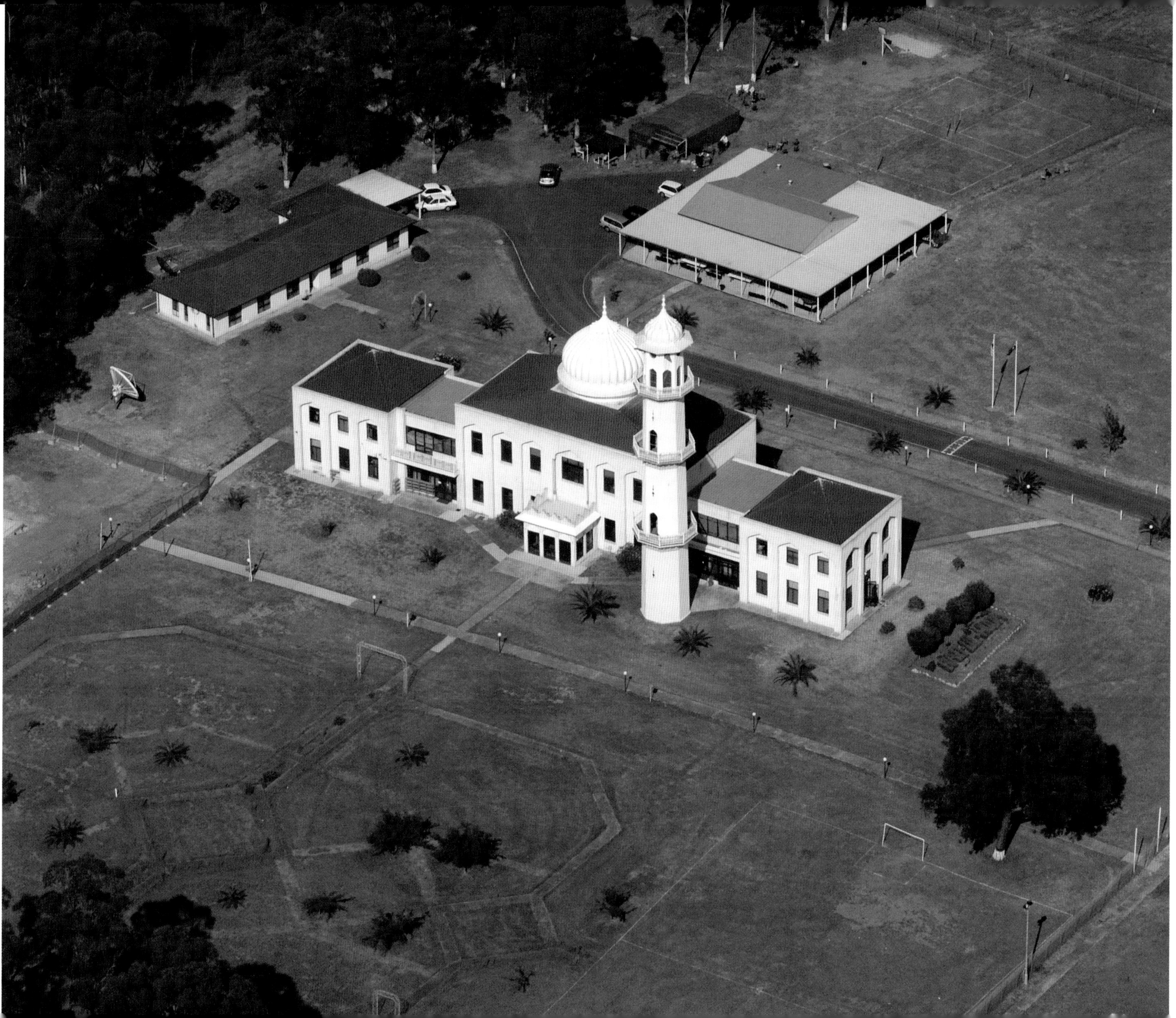

The Pyramid at Olympic Park, Homebush Bay

Modern architecture: a church at Baulkham Hills
Page 174: Brush Farm House, Eastwood, the former residence of
Gregory Blaxland, a prominent figure in early Australian history
Page 175: Disused brickworks in Eastwood

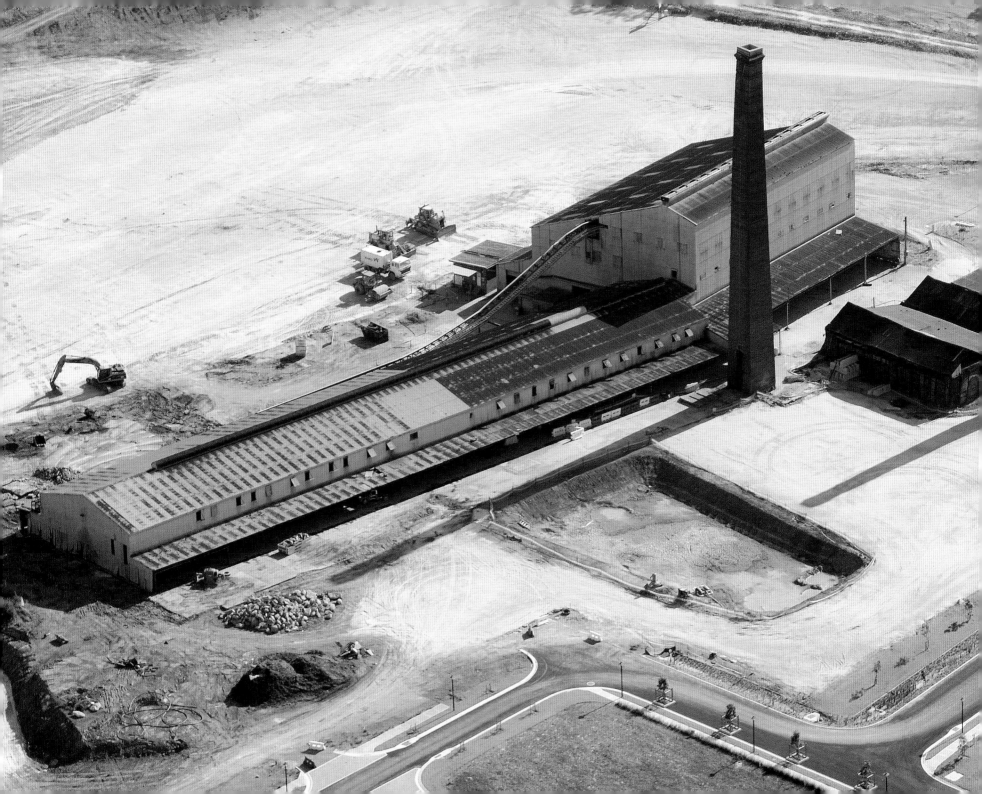

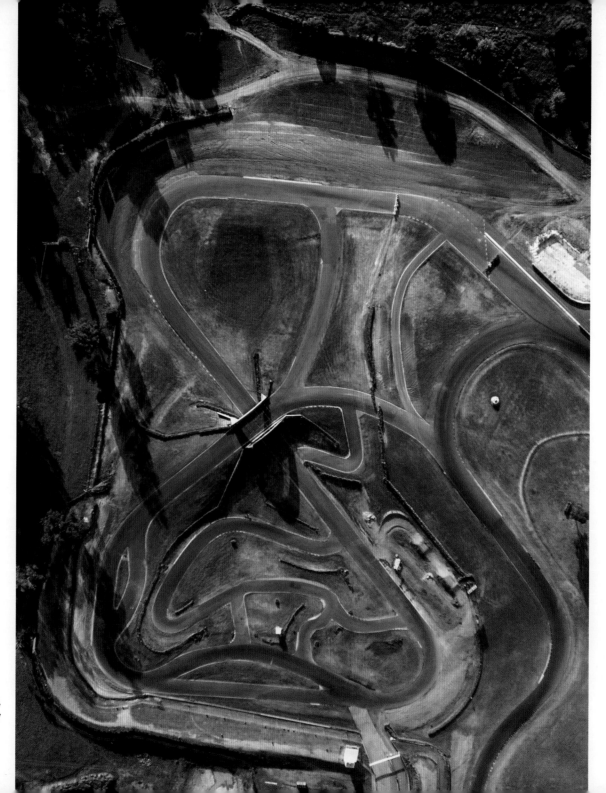

Oran Park Raceway,
west of Sydney

Baha'i Temple, Ingleside

Pages 178–180: Blue Mountains in the misty morning light

Grand Canyon, Blue Mountains

Clouds from over Sydney flowing into the canyons and valleys of Blue Mountains

Three Sisters in the morning mist

Great Canyon from Evans Lookout
Facing page: Grand Canyon, Blue Mountains

Katoomba

The Hydro Majestic Hotel at Medlow Bath

Blue Mountains—the view towards Megalong Valley

Sublime Point at sunset

The Blue Mountains are found approximately 48 km west of Sydney. They are a range of sandstone geological structures that reach to at least 1,190 m . The Blue Mountains are not, as the name suggests, a range of mountains but rather a plateau with rugged eroded gorges of up to depths of 760 m. A large part of the Blue Mountains is incorporated in the Greater Blue Mountains Area World Heritage Site and its constituent seven national parks and a conservation reserve.

The Blue Mountains were thought to be impenetrable by the early white settlers of Sydney, and were not crossed until convicts and other explorers found their way across. The most famous expedition was in 1813, by Blaxland, Wentworth and Lawson. Rather than, like earlier explorers, following the river valleys—only to discover usually that they were terminated by vertical cliffs several hundred metres high—the trio followed the ridges to reach the plateau. This crossing of the Blue Mountains has traditionally been regarded as a critical step that opened the west of New South Wales to European settlement.

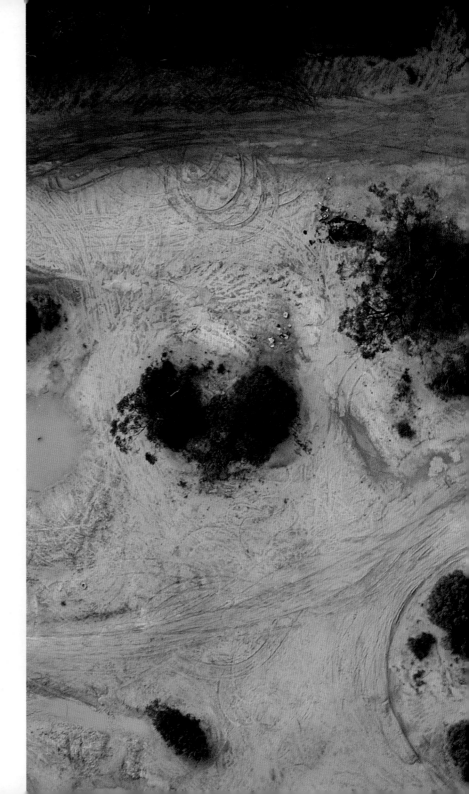

Bare Patch, Blue Mountains National Park

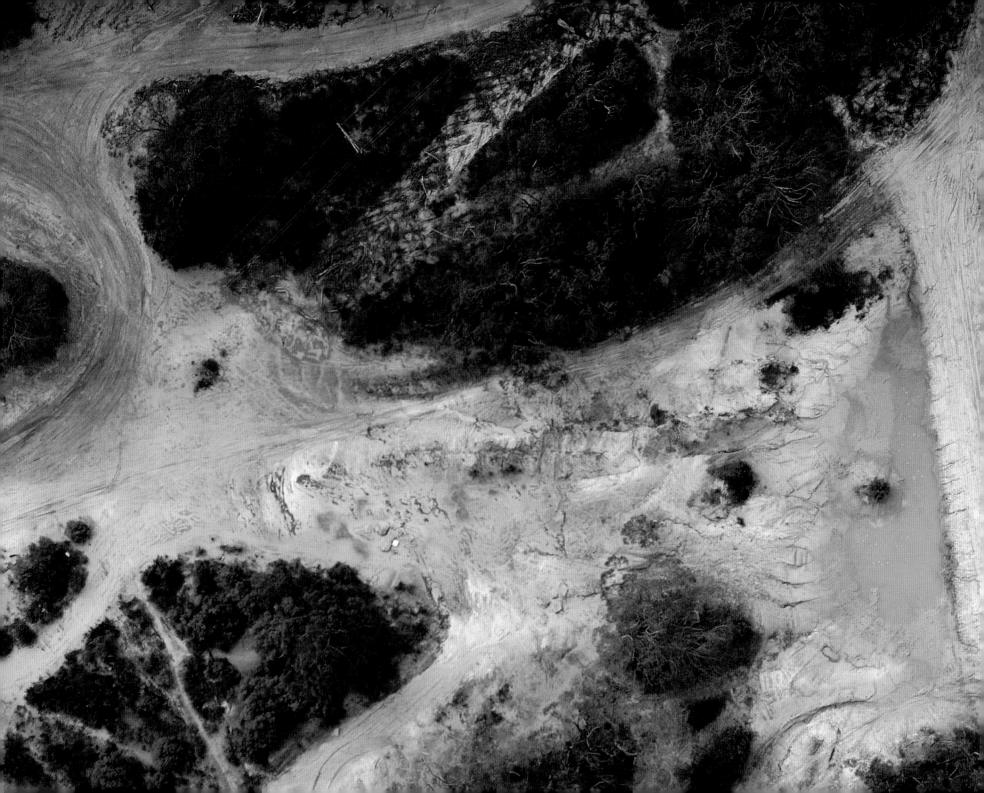

At the back of Kanangra Walls, Kanangra Boyd National Park

Lake Medlow, Blue Mountains National Park

The golden walls of the Grand Canyon, Blue Mountains National Park

Lake Burragorang, a source of water supply for Sydney

Broken Rock Range near Yerranderie,
Kanangra Boyd National Park

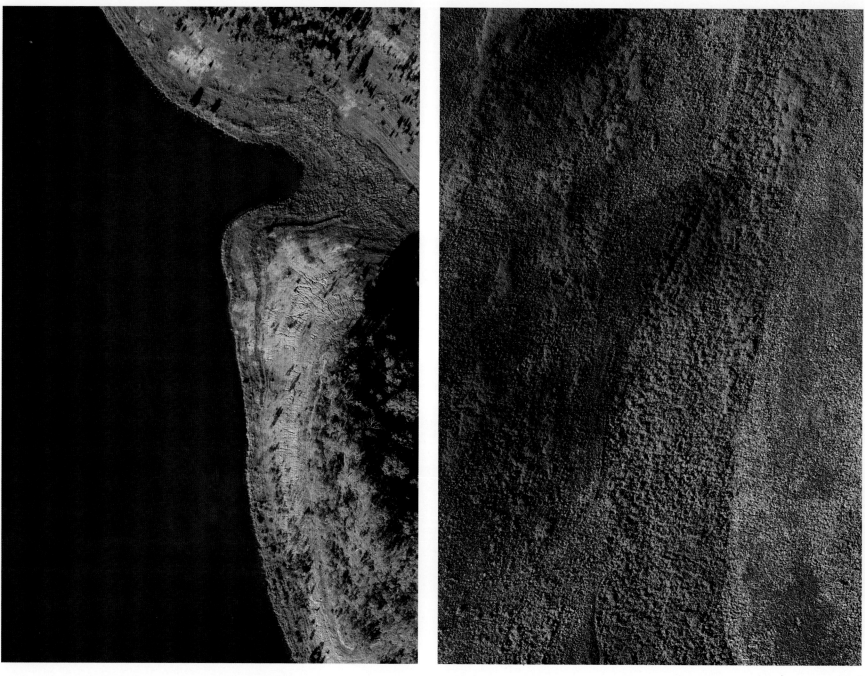

Above and opposite page: Shore patterns at Lake Burragorang

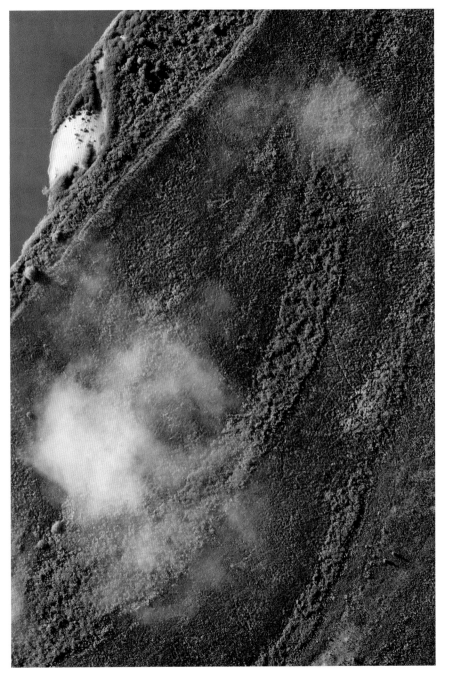

Above and facing page: Broken Rock Range near Yerranderie, Kanangra Boyd National Park

Jamison Valley, Blue Mountains
National Park

The Three Sisters, Katoomba